A BROKEN HEART STILL BEATS

A Collection of Poetry About Heartbreak, Love & Raw Emotions

ANNETTE E. RICHARDS

I hope my book inspires you
Annette E. Richards
April 2021

ISBN: 978-0-578-75959-3 (Paperback)

Any references to historical events, real people, or real places are used fictitiously. Names, characters, and places are products of the author's imagination.

Book design by Chanteé The Designer.

Printed & published by Amazon KDP, Inc.

DEDICATION

First and foremost, I thank Almighty God for making my prison a platform for my purpose. Without Him I am nothing.

To my sweet daughters Anyra and Arianna - This book was birthed from a desolate place that eventually became the platform for each piece of poetry written. I would not be where I am today without you. You both are the air I breathe and continue to be the wind beneath my wings. Thank you for encouraging me to write and embracing the hidden gift of art that was inside me. We've walked this path together, and we never left each other's side. You are amazing women that exemplify fortitude and class. I am so proud of you. You will forever be my sweet daughters.

ACKNOWLEDGEMENTS

To my wonderful mother who has loved me through the heartbreak and has pushed me to higher heights with her unconditional love and support. Thank you for listening to me read my poetry whenever I called. You were always there and listened to every word. Thank you for praying me through the most difficult time of my life and pushing me to see that there would one day be a rainbow after the rain. This book would not have been possible without you. I love you.

To my amazing sisters Stephanie and Jessica who relentlessly stood by my side during the incredibly tough times and who celebrate me today. Your prayers and words of strength and encouragement will forever be remembered. Thank you for always being truthful yet tender and understanding. May God continue to have favor in your lives for everything you poured into my life.

To my dearest cousin and sweetest friend Gwen who always kept it real and helped me to see through a clear lens. You kept me grounded and steeped in reality and at the same time showed tremendous compassion towards me. You held my hand every step of the way and never let go. I will forever be grateful for you.

To Dr. Kara Covington my spiritual mentor who consistently prayed with me and for me and my family. Thank you for the many phone calls at any hour of the day or night and for always taking me to God's word for answers. Thank you for sending me daily devotions and affirmations that I still refer to today. I will forever cherish our friendship. Thank you for standing in the gap for me.

To the woman who saved my life, Ammereta Gaskin, who pushed me when I was ready to deal with life's issues. You are an amazing gift to this world and have been placed here to help others realize their potential and to be the bridge for transformation. I believe we were destined to meet and it goes without saying that I am who I am today because of you.

To my amazing girlfriends who embraced me in insurmountable ways and carefully held my wounded heart in your hands. I am forever grateful for your presence in my life. I will always hold a special place in my heart for each of you.

To my Bestie, LaVern, who also was the wind beneath my wings and pushed me to fly again. You let me cry as long as I needed to but then pushed me to stand tall and to hold my head up like the woman of God I was called to be. I would not have survived without you. Rest in peace my dear friend.

To the Divorce Care leaders at Woodstream Church in Bowie, Maryland, who were instrumental in my healing process. The program was phenomenal and really supported my spiritual growth throughout its duration. Thank you for the tremendous work you do to help thousands of people who are in a season of transition.

To everyone who prayed for me and encouraged me, I appreciate you so much.

table *of* CONTENTS

Chapter 1

The Gloom

Chapter 2

The Dawn

Chapter 1

THE GLOOM

A partial or total darkness; a dark or shadowy place; lowness of spirits; dejection; an atmosphere of despondency.

DEAD BODIES

How many dead bodies were left behind? Not just physically but emotionally too.

Dead bodies who can't speak about it but feel the piercing of their souls everywhere they turn.

Dead bodies who can't move or breathe or see their way through.

Dead bodies who are sleepwalking through life everyday.

Dead bodies whose breath was snatched from them as they ran as fast as they could chasing a dream that was only a dream.

Dead bodies who are collateral damage for the

choices that were made.

Dead bodies who dread the darkness as they hold on to see what the dawn of a new day will bring.

Dead bodies who call out when nobody answers and awaits the day when it will all make sense.

Maybe that day will never come, so the choice is to retreat or rise up and walk in purpose.

How many dead bodies were left behind for the sake of trying to save your own life?

You said you just wanted to live but you really died yourself.

Angry Black Women Don't Talk

Angry black women don't talk. They are quiet as a church mouse running across boards of brokenness while the loud sound of the organ plays drowning out their quiet screams.

They press down their feelings like fresh squeezed orange juice that tastes so sweet but leaves a bitter taste in their mouths after brushing their teeth as they try to brighten their smile when nothing else matters but the thought of how they are perceived by other people.

They smile and laugh in hopes that nobody sees them behind the mask of pretending that they had a good day when really their day was consumed with unwanted thoughts that were hard to tame.

Angry black women don't talk. They bleed from

the deep wounds they feel from an ablation of their hearts but tell themselves that every little thing is gonna be alright as they comb their pretty hair and paint their lips with colors that outshine the darkness covering their mouths. They put on their happy faces in places that don't intimidate them but cover their nakedness.

Every time they feel the anxiety of a vivid image of yesterday, they try to pull that imagination down like a tug of war. Tugging, and at war against their own silence. Sometimes quietly thinking about how they're holding on so tightly to a thick rope but feeling like they're only hanging on by a thin thread.

Anger is for the bitches and crazy black women who don't give a damn. Who speak their piece loud and clear until their voices fade away like a wave within the ocean resting on the shore.

Anger isn't for the pretty ones who walk in their red bottoms that bleed from the pain of emotional abuse suffered at the hand of somebody they sold their soul to. Hell, the pretty ones don't even know what anger looks like. But they know what they taste is like bitter wine and vinegar being handed to them when they say I thirst.

They get even with Steven and the other ones, cause they're angry black women instead of getting even with themselves and realizing that they can't change nobody else.

Hush. Quiet now. Just whisper from the place that hurts so bad that nothing can get rid of it.

Angry black women don't talk. They just keep the peace as they sink deeper into despair; oftentimes screaming, "I'm hurting" without making a sound.

When will they really let their hair down, take off their hoops and trade their red bottoms for white bottoms and stand up for themselves and fight the silence by screaming to the top of their lungs, "I am worthy."

Worthy of love and acceptance and the good life that they've traded for whatever life they've allowed to be handed to them.

The silence is broken as they take a deep breath and love anyway and trust anyway and choose to be happy anyway.

Some angry black women do talk because I am one of them.

Let the Real Church Say Amen

The Church... What is it? Who is it?
Where is it when you need it?

Hurt feels like muddy waters when you can only see your reflection through the soot and ashes that burned a hole in your soul.

Life doesn't stop for the preacher man and his family who are at the 4th of July picnic when you're wondering if your family will make it to Thanksgiving without falling apart.

Is marriage really easy when couples are dying and people are crying while they sit on long pew rows next to the very one who shames them at home when the church doors close?

Going to church on Sunday morning saying,

"Amen" and then bible study on Wednesday night, somehow turned into Friday night beat downs and saying anything out the mouth to tear a sister down to only repeat the cycle on Sunday morning again.

On every corner you see it and read the signs that speak of loving your neighbor when you don't even love yourself. The doors of the church are open but close at midnight when the doorknobs of life hit you where the good Lord split you and you're afraid to sit down because of the pain.

People say the church is within, but there's nothing within when your soul is invisible and nobody seems to care about what you're going through. The first family is really the last family you expected to allow their joy to override your misery that doesn't have any company to love.

The church members are brothers and sisters who are bleeding out themselves but put band-aids over their own scars before they put on their Sunday best so their clothes don't get dirty.

Where does my soul find refuge? Not in a church but in God who knows all, sees all, hears all and loves all no matter what your scars look like.

And now unto Him who caught me in His arms after falling head first off the cliff of hopelessness.

Let the preacher man, the brothers and sisters and even the unbelievers stand back and watch the Creator do His best work and then the real church will surely say "Amen."

This Makes No Sense

Scratching my head everyday wondering if I'm supposed to be in this place.

This place, that place, every place seems to be closing in on me.

The walls of my understanding are like pillars too high to climb to see the mountaintop.

The valley is so deep that climbing up out of it seems insurmountable.

What do my hands say that can't feel you no more?

My eyes soak my face with tears all day for any reason.

My ears hear the sweet-talking, mean-talking, self-talking recorder that seems to push play on its own.

I taste the bitter and sweet kool-aid of life, each glass reflecting the color of a rainbow sent from heaven.

I smell your sexy cologne as I think about your charisma out there but in here the smell of hatred permeates.

My senses can make no sense of what will never make sense.

The unanswered questions perplex my mind but my spirit holds me and rocks me to sleep at night.

Having faith makes no sense, believing makes no sense, hoping makes no sense.

Scratching my head everyday wondering if I'm supposed to be in this place cause none of this makes sense.

Open Heart Surgery

Surgery had been scheduled long before she realized when bomb day would come but he knew.

She said her prayers before she went to sleep that night not knowing that she would awaken to a different world that wasn't ready for the news that this time it would be her.

The surgeon scrubbed in and washed his hands of everything that once existed.

He put on his scrubs and walked into the operating room one last time.

The room was still and cold but it didn't matter to him because he had done this surgery before.

This time was different though as he asked for the

scalpel but knew there was no anesthesia to numb the pain.

He cut into her chest where he found her broken heart.

He held it in his hands and kissed it goodbye because he knew he would never see it again.

But there was another surgeon there too, who refused to let her die.

So He took her heart out of the hands of a man who didn't deserve it and gently placed it back into her chest.

He numbed her body and said I love you but this is going to hurt, as He tried to prepare her for what was to come.

The scalpel He used tore her heart completely but she knew He meant it for good and not for evil.

You see, open-heart surgery was necessary so that she could live again with a new one.

A new heart that forgives every injustice done.

A new heart that loves everyday it is allowed to beat.

A new heart that will one day love someone else.

From His Perspective

As a man thinketh in his heart so is he.

What was his heart thinking all this time?

His mouth was silent as the routine of life would soon whisper sweet nothings in his ear.

Something was wrong but my analytical self couldn't figure it out.

I don't think he really knew either so he convinced himself that life was like a box of chocolates.

He slowly ate his favorite piece to savor the sweet taste of a love that was slipping through his fingertips.

He held on as long as he could but the blinding

darkness swept him into a never ending tornado.

The damage was already done, as the debris fell from a pickup truck turned on its side.

He was a dead man walking into places he had no business going.

His heart knew better, but he was blinded by a deceitful world wrapped in a big red bow of loneliness.

His anger and the hurt he felt were real too ,but he locked the door of his heart and burned the key.

Blaming and shaming was the game he played when the hand he was dealt was empty promises that felt like a dream come true.

The longer the walk, the darker the road as a soul

who once knew the Father only knew Him from a distance now.

His people still prayed for the day he would surrender his life for the abundant one he was promised where love was deep, real and sure.

The only love that could fill the deep dark hole of nothingness medicated by a counterfeit life that replaced the real one he once had.

His new life looked good from the outside as he traveled the friendly skies to rewrite history so it would all make sense at least to him.

The silence still speaks and no one will ever fully understand the perspective of a man they don't know anymore.

Why Do I Still Love You?

I look through the rose colored glasses of ashes that remain from what felt like cigarette burns all over my body.

And I ask myself, why do I still love you?

I loved you forever, but one too many times and three strikes you're out.

Why do I still love you when you broke my heart into pieces like a puzzle that couldn't be put back together?

Not just my pieces, but their pieces too.

"Let Freedom Ring" said the preacher man but it ain't no freedom when you're locked up in your mind and wonder if you'll ever get out of this prison.

Why do I still love you?

I love the air you breathe, the talk you talk and the way your pants move in the wind when you walk towards me and away from me repeating the vicious cycle of loneliness.

Why do I still love you?

Your heart was made of gold and was peaceful like a river flowing from a good place, and I wondered if love could ever be like that again.

Why do I still love you when the heart that used to beat for me is beating for someone else now?

She Will Never Be Me

Lonely I sit by the pool kicking my feet briskly through the water silently screaming for a chance to understand how she became me or was she a reflection of you?

The pain that filled your eyes thrust your desire to escape the finer things of life and drew you like a bee to honey.

You ran as fast as you could like a speeding bullet through my chest and fell in the arms of a sounding board that listened to your disappointments soaking each one of them up.

The emotional bond that followed ripped our hearts apart and the two that became one were no longer.

Low self-esteem, but she was esteemed high above

the cloud of witnesses standing by watching.

Two broken souls deceitfully tied together like the knots in my stomach that won't go away.

Listening to every hurt, and smoothing balm over the wounds that she had no business tending to either.

Rewriting history was easier than seeing the mess that was created by the lies spewed out of the mouths of those that tasted sweet strawberries at the expense of the pain that fed others.

Beautiful brown skin but living in sin; choices to make spinning around in the chaos of your mind.

Triangulation overtook your desire to do the right thing and you made your choice.

But she will never be me.

Pretender

Why pretend that you ever loved me when it's vividly clear that you really only loved the person you see in the mirror.

I Could Hardly Breathe

Desperation was my middle name as I wanted life to be so different but it wasn't giving me what I wanted so desperately.

Life knocked the wind out of me sideways as I lay on the cold hardwood floor of another day.

How could this be?

This was not the life God promised me way back then when I bent over backwards and now half my life is gone.

I tried to stop the hands of time and slow this roller coaster down cause it was moving too fast.

I lost who I was to a camouflaged preferred self only to learn that no self was good enough.

Couldn't get out of bed for dead was what I was feeling inside as I tried to pull my frail silhouette together but inferiority overtook me.

What did I do to deserve this after all I did to preserve this?

I had to dig myself out of this hole but knew I couldn't do it by myself.

So I lifted my hands to a God who I knew was there.

He reached down and pulled me into His bosom and said I'm here, just breathe my child.

I will never leave you nor forsake you like the world of circus animals that jump through hoops for a good laugh.

I woke up from this nightmare with sweaty palms

and a heart racing faster than horses pulling a chariot.

I pinched myself and it really hurt because I realized it was happening for real.

The Thing

The thing reaches to the depths of your soul and it's nothing you can do about it.

The thing is like a thirsty savage after your blood and your generation who nobody knows yet.

The thing rips families apart leaving a puddle of everybody's tears, including grandfather's who wept at the news that he thought he would never hear.

The thing is like a roller coaster ride with twists and turns that jerks you around as you panic.

The thing breaks the heart of people who really care, and are not consumed with their own stuff.

The thing is like a ship sailing through the night in

a treacherous storm that won't stop.

The thing comes to kill, steal and destroy everything in its path, and it doesn't care who it takes down with it.

The thing came after me with a vengeance, and I ran as fast as I could, but it caught me and bit me like a vampire in the darkest of nights.

The coffin was shut this time forever and another one bites the dust.

Can't Take No More

My soul cries out till it can't no more.

My broken heart aches till it can't beat no more.

My tears fall like running water that won't stop no more.

My head spins like a merry-go-round till I can't see straight no more.

My mind ruminates on what's so wrong here till I can't think no more.

Can't catch a break before another tornado hits hard and knocks me down as I try to breathe a slow deep breath of freedom and peace again.

Life's gotta get better soon cause I can't take no more.

Ashamed

Ashamed of what I look like now.

Ashamed of how others see me.

Ashamed of the way he left me.

Ashamed of how people who used to be my friends
treat me.

Ashamed that relationships are broken.

Ashamed that other people have to hurt.

Ashamed of what others know that I don't.

Ashamed that family is an afterthought.

Ashamed of the failure.

Ashamed of my past mistakes.

Ashamed of the emotional abuse.

Ashamed of people laughing at me.

Ashamed of not knowing who I am anymore.

Ashamed of what my children think of me.

Ashamed of how the church folks see me.

Ashamed of losing everything.

Ashamed of how he treated me.

Ashamed of being ashamed.

Uncovered Scars

Blemishes marked

Purple dark

Skies blue

Dark through

Eyes red

Tears wet

Wounds fresh

Scars real

Heart broken

Family hurting

Unfulfilled dreams

Laughter silenced

Marked blemishes

Dark purple

Blue skies

Through dark

Red eyes

Wet tears

Fresh wounds

Real scars

Broken heart

Hurting family

Dreams unfulfilled

Silenced laughter

Scars uncovered

The Palace

The king was in the palace sitting on his mighty throne while the queen enjoyed the good life and the princesses did too.

They bowed and curtsied at the dinner table while the world watched and loved what it saw.

People judging and criticizing based on how their own lives measured up as many of them envied the royal court.

The king so strong and mighty ruled his palace with soft lips but an iron fist as the onlookers said, “Oh, how lovely it must be to be them.”

The popularity contest was never ending as everywhere they went he was known in the gates.

The queen brilliantly dressed in the finest of linens taking care of everybody's business but forsaking her own.

The palace was beautiful as doors swung on gold hinges but every door wasn't shut leaving a crack for the real life to seep in.

The Queen was always on her toes but nobody knows she was blinded by the rose colored glasses she wore adorning her beautiful caramel face.

She was brilliant and broke the glass ceiling as she reached for the stars that she worked so hard to be amongst; educated and free to express herself.

The princesses were so perfect as they wore the finest of linens too with beautiful long silky hair as they held their heads high.

Walking through life sometimes feeling compelled to make excuses for who they were in exchange for the reality that they were fearfully and wonderfully made by God Himself.

They had the perfect lives which was what the queen lived for, oftentimes forsaking herself so that they would experience the life that she never had.

The beautiful little princesses grew to be wonderful women who saw life through the color of the choices they would make themselves.

The queen could no longer protect them as she begged for the life that they all once had.

And one glistening summer's eve the king mounted his horse and trotted out the door of a good life in exchange for what he thought was a better one.

The queen lost the very essence of her soul, playing Russian Roulette in the game of life hoping the pain would soon end.

The princesses found their own castles and sang sweet songs and wore fine linen dresses that they handmade themselves this time, while the king and queen watched from afar.

Soon the queen's heart grew happy again, and she waltzed back into the ballroom of life and prepared a feast for her princesses and the generations that would spring forth.

Long live the king, the queen and their princesses as the palace still stood after the wreckage, and they lived happily ever after in a new world filled with love and blessings.

Pride Will Kill You

The ego ran away and left the true self, the self that nobody sees but you when you look in the mirror as the shame covers you like a dark cloud hanging over your life.

The choice was yours to make all along and I applaud you for talking about self-preservation at the expense of other's devastation as you walked out the revolving door never to return.

They say pride comes before a fall; so you took a leap of faith into the deepest darkest hole where you had never been before.

Anger gripped your soul as your nostrils pulsated in and out at the very site of me.

What a man thinks in his heart so is he they also say.

So what was your heart thinking all this time when nobody knew but you that you were dying inside.

I won't take the blame for a life that wasn't mine as a child but became mine when I said I do to you and the heavy baggage that I didn't know I'd be carrying.

Oh my luggage was just as heavy as I toted Louis Vuitton down the red carpet but life was really like Walmart which was just as good if only I understood what I know now.

Many sessions that went left when they were supposed to go right with really no intention of changing but saving face for a world who knew a different you.

Pride will kill you.

Kill the very essence of your soul.

Kill your dreams at night and visions in the light.

Kill your future with the ones you say you love.

Kill your motivation, inspiration and desperation for changing what you really might want to but pride got in the way.

Now walking down the long green mile to the end of an existence you once knew.

Determined to make what's so wrong so right cause you gotta prove something to the grown man while still dealing with the little boy inside.

But Pride won't let you talk about it with the same people who got just as many flaws as you do.

It was always something else trying to deflect the real root of the tree to me, as I stood like a tree planted by the river of the fiery darts that were coming my way.

Something has got to give but pride wants to live and so it does happily ever after by itself.

My Sentiments

Lost in a love that I never really had.

The universe joined our souls then locked the door of our hearts and we threw away the key.

For what?

A misunderstanding that left my thoughts paralyzed with wondering what I had done to deserve this.

You seemed like a nice gentleman who swept me off my feet like black butterflies spreading their wings.

Forever didn't come for us like the beautiful songs that we shared said it would.

How could we emerge with boundaries suffocating our deep feelings?

I'll never truly know because you dropped a bomb on me that detonated my heart and destroyed our relationship forever.

You seemed so sure but this masquerade turned into a foolish game that only you were playing.

You walked away from something really good and the future of generations to come and I'm disappointed.

You are not the man you used to be, so who are you really?

Broken Promises

Promises are to be kept and not abandoned by walking down a dark alley that led to a dead end.

A dead end to the shaming and blaming of somebody who was out for blood forgetting that he had been given pints for his own survival.

Her mind was like a merry-go-round and couldn't contain thoughts of another woman holding his hand when he never held hers.

Her stomach ached at the thought of his brown skin caressing the skin of a secret lover that didn't look like her.

She cringed at the only vision she saw when she closed her eyes to the world in the middle of the day and heard his favorite song.

She tried not to hate when she was told to turn the other cheek but there weren't any other cheeks to turn.

No more salted tears running down her face as she couldn't make sense of it all and felt drained like a bathtub full of hopelessness.

She dreaded the very thought of him driving Miss Daisy in a fast and furious sports car that she didn't see coming.

She was hurt beyond what was thinkable, and he never bothered to make it right because empathy wasn't knocking on his door.

Promises were broken and lives were shattered but he kept walking through the glass with bruises that he pretended not to see.

The ultimate promise was broken as he sold his soul to the devil for a nonrefundable ticket to the sideshow of a counterfeit life with someone else.

No More

No, I won't stand idly by and let you use me like a rental car that you turn in after you're done with it.

No, I won't be used like a new pair of shoes that look good when you first wear them but get scuff marks after they've been kicked around.

No, I won't be pulled in when you need me to help solve the problems of this world but I'm left with my own problems to solve as you turn your back on me.

No, you can't have my soul, mind and love only when you want them and throw confetti in my face when life is good for you and now terrible for me because you walked out.

No, I won't settle no more for being a garbage can when I know there's peace like a river awaiting me as I cross the red sea of sacrifices made and a broken heart.

No, I won't cover up and make excuses for things that go wrong when they could have gone right if only your ears listened and your heart understood.

No, I won't carry the heavy burden of everybody else's stuff and live my life burdened with baggage that don't even belong to me.

No, I scream in the darkness at night when I can't see my way out of this only to realize that my love runs deep like a river that has no end.

So how do I turn this situation around so that my heart isn't heavy with the burden of loving you?

I say yes, I will love in spite of misunderstandings and eyes rolling to the back of your head when the days are dark and the moments are lonely.

Yes, I will set boundaries and rules that will help us dance to a rhythm of the same beat that will play forever in our minds when distance is only miles away.

Yes, I will pray for you and let you go into a cold world where the warmth of my love will forever be there when you run back into my arms.

Yes, I will love hard and love more and love you from afar as long as we both shall live.

She Was Only Two

What did she do when the life she always knew felt like the darkness seen when she closed her eyes and couldn't remember anything.

She arose everyday to play with other girls who she thought were just like her but she really didn't know their story; nor did they know hers.

At two, what did she do when reaching for her favorite toys was like fun on the waves of what she would later learn to be despair.

At two, who knew that life would forever change when all she wanted to do was play with her baby dolls and comb their hair.

As she grew up, she created a life that appeared to be satisfying but she was empty like a sump pump running out of water.

She was beautiful on the outside but always somehow felt ugly on the inside not realizing that her insides were compromised many years ago.

She desperately tried to remember her childhood that was blocked like a police line during a protest.

She shrugged her shoulders and lived her life not understanding how she could forget who taught her how to ride a bike or who her favorite elementary school teacher was.

Over the years, the desperate little girl within her chose the finer things of life that she thought would fill the deep void that only truth could reveal.

So, the little girl now a grown woman sat across the table from her mother who answered the multiple choice test of life that was circumvented when she had no choice in the matter.

A perplexed mother who didn't know to look for help back then as the generational curse of abuse was minimized to overemphasize the ignorance that society embraced.

She had heard this story before but this time she opened her eyes to the reality that would heal her wounded soul forever.

You see, she was only two when her innocence was stolen and while there was no penetration, the violation stole the sun out of her shine and the colorful rainbow out of her sky.

But she chose to scream through the pain and dig herself out of the deepest valley to find the pearl that rests in the depths of her and live freely.

Flood of Memories

I stood in the middle of nowhere and couldn't believe what I was seeing.

The worst was yet to come when my sweet 16 and graduation memories lay on a wet floor of shadows.

I was so numb and wanted to ball up in a corner and cry till no more tears came.

The emptiness I felt inside is unexplainable because nobody has been through what I have in a million years.

Years of times past run across my feeble mind as I toss those things I so desperately want to hang onto into the sea of never forgetting.

All I could save was sweet baby girl's footprints

and memoirs from Paris that I will always cherish.

Loss is tangible but life is precious like sweet,
sweet memories.

Letting go of each one as I rock myself to sleep as I
pray for the dawn of a new day.

Chapter 2

THE DAWN

The first appearance of light in the sky before sunrise; the beginning of a phenomenon or period of time, especially one considered favorable.

The Dawn

I awaken to the sun with bright brown eyes as I see the dawn of a new day.

A day filled with possibilities and probabilities that I ain't never seen before.

A day so rich with chocolate milk, and I see the sun again.

The beautiful bright sun that reminds me of walking in the rain with the one I love but all alone in the sink hole that crashed through my mornings not that long ago.

The dawn of a new day, a new me that I see through the crystal ball telling me that the life ahead will be better than the one behind.

Birds chirping like the sweet sound of music that I longed to hear when I couldn't hear nothing but the chatter in my head making so much noise that I couldn't hear myself think.

The sun is shining bright like a new penny found in the sand on the beach of my waves, coming into shore where there's love and laughter and the soft sweet wind on a beautiful summer night glistening against the calm seas like the life I'm living now.

Calm like peace be still where the waves cease and the wind stops and the roses smell like honeysuckle and life seems real again.

The tide has turned and life is sweet like a peanut butter surprise with a cherry on top.

I can see the dawn of a new day and it's beautiful.

The ATL

They sat around the kitchen table like four generations shooting the breeze while drinking Simply Lemonade.

Peanut butter crackers with jelly at 1 o'clock in the morning when she couldn't sleep tasted so good when life tasted so bitter.

Best friend dreaming of acting and she's young gifted and black and beautiful and determined to make it to the life God created for her to live.

Baby girl was so beautiful too as she found her new wings on top of a pyramid standing tall and cheering to her own rhythm.

Momma got a new pair of shoes that took her out to dinner but wasn't the mister she hoped for, but

Prince Charming was out there somewhere ready to love the sweet spirit of the woman she was.

Momma's children meant everything to her, and she was also included in that number when many a night she bowed her head to pray before she went to sleep but couldn't.

She stumbled to the kitchen only to meet her at the table and cried many tears that a Thin Oreo cookie helped to sooth.

Why did she have to leave a bleeding family behind, feeling guilty but happy at the same time?

So she wouldn't have to deal with running into the very soul who stole hers.

She was bleeding out like a river but was being saved by the Almighty as she was stealing away for healing the pain of yesterday, today and forever more.

Stronger, wiser, better each day in the ATL.

A New Birth took place as she arose from a baptism that freed her soul from misery and turned her frown into a smile.

A smile that was brighter and adorned with her favorite red lipstick as tears of freedom fell from her cheeks into her favorite glass of Moscato wine.

The ATL was the place that saved her dying soul as they sat around the kitchen table like four generations shooting the breeze while drinking Simply Lemonade.

The Perfect Ending

The end is the beginning of a new life
filled with mind shifts through a maze of broken
pieces of glass put back together.

I see the whole picture now which was once skewed
by what only I wanted to see.

The puzzle pieces are perfectly aligned and life
feels good again.

The cloud of raindrops that flood my face are sweet
caramel salty tears that express the joy my heart
feels inside.

Life was bitter but is sweeter, different and new.

Spreading my own wings now which were once
clipped so I couldn't fly.

I'm a survivor and I'm still here seeing new horizons and flying high over every valley and mountain that once stood in my way.

So the end is the beginning of a new life filled with sunny mornings and fresh coffee and bubble baths.

I now dance to a new rhythm that is so rich and beautiful and perfect.

Breakfast

Good morning beautiful sunshine so sunny and bright like warm sand between my toes in a land far away where the wind is crisp and clean like tomorrow.

Take me there as my imagination runs wild with pleasantries that speak hope and freedom and life.

Early in the morning when I rise I feel hypnotized by sunny skies with clouds that penetrate the air I breathe when life is wonderful and new.

Chocolate covered strawberries melt in my mouth as I indulge in what tastes good and covers my soul with browness that's free to live with no hangups created by me, myself and I.

I am free to be me and feel good in the skin that I'm

in as I dance to my favorite melody.

I've never heard this song before but it sings to my heart a quiet rhythm of certainty and confidence.

Good morning beautiful sunshine so sunny and bright like my favorite breakfast in my favorite place where warm sand highlights my cheekbones as I lay here naked and peaceful.

Transformation

Like butterflies who spread their wings and land on dew dripped leaves on a bright sunny morning.

Like butterflies who sleep long dark nights bouncing off walls that surround them like a tsunami.

Like butterflies who were birthed out of a generational curse that tried to clip their wings so that they could never fly.

Like butterflies who looked in the mirror and saw beautiful brown eyes with dark circles from the dark clouds hiding their pain.

Like butterflies who people pleased and everybody teased because they really wanted to be like her.

Like butterflies strong and brave whose wings

were repeatedly clipped leaving the smell of rose petals trailing behind.

Like butterflies determined to make it but break it every time they leave the cocoon of life on a rainy day.

Like butterflies who fly high above valleys and snow covered mountain tops dripping with sweet smelling honey.

Like butterflies who believed they could make it as they spread their beautiful wings of every beautiful color under the sun.

Like butterflies who soar amongst the eagles strong, mighty and free.

Free to dance, free to love, free to be who they really are.

Beautiful Wings Again

Wings so beautiful and tall spread out like a prism of many colors.

Colors that reflect the seasons of life as darkness is overcome by peace and love and bright sunny skies filled with bursts of happiness.

Teeth so white from a beautiful smile seen again, where there's no space for worry but only for good vibes and good love that you deserve.

Spirits lifted by the hands of love that hold you as you fly with your own wings and live your own life.

Beautiful wings that are as strong and resilient as an eagle's that soar high and wide and free.
Fly high like breathtaking rainbows and sing songs that make you happy and free like bright sparkly

colors that make you smile.

I See What You Can't

I see the dark circles around your eyes full of hope.

Hoping and wishing that things would be what your heart remembers from yesterday but yesterday is today and things are the same.

I see snowflakes and happiness and the color purple that used to make your soul dance.

I see fear gripping so tightly as you say goodbye to the little girl and hello to the woman you're staring at in the mirror of the unknown.

I see freedom as you let her go and walk down the dark alley that appears to have no end.

But there is a plan that you must embrace that's bigger than your own, full of sparkling lights and milk and honey.

I see the promise land that awaits you no matter what detours are taken.

I will be there at the end when you fall into His grace and my open arms full of love.

I Am

I Am...a child of God

I Am...a survivor

I Am...courageous

I Am...brave

I Am...loyal

I Am...authentic

I Am...who God says I am

I Am...worthy of love

I Am...strong

I Am...smart

I Am...healed

I Am...whole

I Am...a good friend

I Am...independent

I Am...happy

I Am...a legacy lover

I Am...good enough

I Am...valued

I Am...confident

I Am...a great mom

I Am...caring

I Am...kind

I Am...classy

I Am...a glass half full girl

I Am...me

Chemistry

My beautiful brown eyes were heavy as I wondered what life was like for him during these lonely days of mine.

Moving fast to the beat of a rhythm I was afraid to face alone but he was constantly in my dreams.

The rhythm of his heart danced for me too but was uncertain because sweet love had been camouflaged by fear of the unknown.

Chemistry introduced two souls that collided into one that felt good and safe and yet left them both wondering, "Where do we go from here?"

Higher Heights

He chose what he thought was happiness while raking his bloodline over the coals for his so-called self-preservation.

He ripped out the core of humanness and tried to replace it with frivolous antics that were temporary as a band-aid.

He left generations looking for love in places that they had no business.

Places that were as dark as the sin he was in.

People silently cringed at the thought of who he had become .

A charismatic stranger who could fool the best of them but not the Almighty who knew the number of hairs on his head because He made them all.

The journey of generations had been filled with thistles and thorny bushes that have left bruised heels, crushed souls and unhealed scars.

But the promise of beauty for ashes spoke loudly from the mountain top of despair, and since God is within them they did not fail.

They rose to higher heights breaking soul ties and generational curses that no longer have power over them.

Gratefulness

I'm so grateful for the everlasting love of a good Father who knows the inner parts of me and still says I do.

He tells me I love you more than you can ever imagine when you close your eyes and can't see beyond your circumstance.

His still voice whispers in my ear "My love flows deeper than your wounds like salve to soothe your broken bones."

I'm so grateful for a Daddy who won't ever leave me or forsake me like humans with corrupted hearts that are polluted from sin.

Sin that ensnares them like a rope hanging from a tree after throwing a hand grenade as hard as they can because they don't know what else to do.

I am so grateful for the perfect hands of a Father who promised to fight for me so that I could have victory every day I choose to.

You see, His hands have nail scars to prove the fight was already fixed as He knew me before the world did and said, "Child you belong to me."

With faith as small as a mustard seed I believed everything He told me and my heart grew bigger and could love better than it ever did before.

I'm so grateful that we will meet face-to-face one day as I await those words when He welcomes me home where no death can do us part.

Until then, I will show Him gratitude now by lifting my hands in praise as gratefulness flows from my

heart while my legacy watches and takes on the
same posture as they also say “I’m grateful.”

Time Stood Still

Time stood still today as I quickly gasped for air to fill my empty lungs that couldn't breathe no more.

Breathless to say the least as I people watched and discovered my life ain't no different than nobody else's.

The same pain I felt I saw on the faces of others, and I counted each blessing that belonged to me.

I stood on the ledge of life and jumped on the shoulders of other giants who were never defeated by Goliath.

The winds have settled down now and the moonlight shines brightly across this side of town and I can breathe again.

As free and as tall as a cemented lamppost once dimmed by adversity, but brightness will always cover the darkness of yesterday.

The weight has been lifted and nothing temporary is permanent.

The sun is shining again and it's beautiful like Easter lilies on Resurrection Sunday.

Time stood still today but the clock is still ticking... tick tock, tick tock.

Come See About Me

Come see about this lonely heart wrapped in silver confetti waiting to be surprised with sounds of love.

Sounds of whispers nibbling on my ear waiting to hear you're safe and special and mine.

Spoon me at 3 a.m. when that's all I want inside.

To be touched, held and loved with no strings attached and no rules that hinder this special thing.

Come see about me and show me all of who you are so I can see through the windows of your soul and stroke you where it used to hurt.

Taste me and tell me how I make you smile like your favorite ice cream that you can't wait to have.

Come see what beautiful rainbows tomorrow will
unfold and I'll come see about you forever.

I Remember You

My heart raced as I could hear your silent voice whispering to me in the darkness.

My soul danced to a familiar rhythm as it was awakened by feelings of beautiful butterflies that were still there.

My mind couldn't comprehend living life without you, and thoughts overtook my world like waves crashing against the shore leaving me fragile.

The invisible bond stretched a thousand miles away, and I looked in the rear view mirror of life and longed for the day I would hear you say, "I remember you."

The walls of fear no longer have a place here, and the chance for romance is sweet like honeysuckle and pink raindrops that you kiss away.

Shadows of my past slowly fade away as I breathe freely and completely and give way to trust.

I choose to run towards love that is blue like skies, sweet like cherries and beautiful like rainbows because I remember you too.

My Black Skin Matters

My black skin matters in a world that says it doesn't.

Chocolate oceans of waves rising to the shore of a movement that will change our lives forever come crashing into whiteness that tries to keep them at bay.

Brown dimples permeate the smiles of a generation that comes from my bosom, as I see innocent faces that see life as easy and sweet as they should.

They have not yet been shaped by the ignorance of others whose intent is to render them powerless, and they won't ever be by the power vested in them and me.

My daughters' brown beautiful skin radiates a

glimmer of hope as they see the world through the eyes that helped shape their belief systems and continues to encourage them to be strong and beautiful.

My people are hurting as they rise to new heights that still try to tell them they don't matter, but they really know they do, now more than ever before.

Eyes are bleeding tears that long for a quiet peaceful world that acknowledges me and you and them.

Our lives speak to a nation that's opening its eyes to the unnecessary bloodshed of our black brothers and sisters.

Our power matters as we make it known that we are here, and we won't ever turn back to a life of slavery that our ancestors lived as we stand on their shoulders tall and free.

We are black. We are beautiful. We are here, and our black skin matters too.

God Took A Picture of Me Today

It was the perfect picture of beautiful rainbows plummeting the sky falling to a desolate world full of hatred and love and crooked smiles.

Crooked smiles that decide each day how to live with open hearts as God sees them in a timeless earth.

An earth full of laughter that fills the soul and illuminates the sunshine within.

God took a picture of me today, and He saw a beautiful orchid standing tall and firm and beautiful but not perfect.

He saw music and bright colored shadows dancing in the streets of New Orleans gripping their purple beads exuding royalty.

He saw eyes that spoke to the pain within and a heart that stood still to a beating drum suddenly stopped.

He saw motherless and fatherless children riding the merry-go-round of life and death which are in the power of your tongue.

He saw watercolored lilies dancing with raindrops of honeysuckle in the Garden of Eden.

He saw images of Himself in you and me as the picture slowly developed its character in the dark room of life filled with winding roads and mountains and cool waterfalls over a cliff of despair.

God took a picture of me today and my eyes were surprised to see Him instead of the old me I once knew.

The perfect picture was also flawed by the blood stained hands that reached down to pick me up from a place that wasn't my home anymore.

The picture reflected the sunlight of His eyes and the warmth of His heart; and I could live and breathe again, but this time totally in Him.

If God took a picture of you today, what would He see?

Only you know.

A Broken Heart Still Beats

A broken heart still beats for a love it once felt many years ago when you waltzed into a quiet life that one day dreamed of loving and being loved unconditionally.

It now dreams of the sweet smell of love on a summer night as the white sand presses between my toes as I skip along the boardwalk of a new life.

A life that promises to be better than that one ever was as the hands of time move swiftly into a new chapter on the journey of this one.

A chapter full of newness and warmth from the sun I thought I'd never see again.

Now I see it rising as my heart still beats like a drum that will play a different song forever.

A broken heart still beats, as the stitches from switches that bruised my soul are mended back together by time and a dose of the future.

A future filled with beautiful choices as each one proves to erase those that were handed to me.

A broken heart still beats as two became one on the dawn of a new life filled with possibilities and opportunities that have never been realized.

Exhale as you breathe to a new rhythm that's sweet and tender like the life I once dreamed of where I would love and be loved unconditionally.

Beat on broken heart until you clap your hands to a new sound, dance to a new song, and until you choose to love again.

Made in the USA
Middletown, DE
16 April 2021

37698804R00060